A BOOK OF PRAISES

by Joyce Blackburn

Illustrations by Martha Bentley

ZONDERVAN
PUBLISHING HOUSE
OF THE ZONDERVAN CORPORATION
GRAND RAPIDS, MICHIGAN 49506

A BOOK OF PRAISES
Copyright © 1980 by Joyce Blackburn

Library of Congress Cataloging in Publication Data

Blackburn, Joyce.
    A book of praises.

     1. Praise of God.   2. Meditations.   I.   Title.
BV4817.B53   242   80-21787
ISBN 0-310-42061-X

Edited by Judith E. Markham
Designed by Judith E. Markham and
Martha Bentley

Printed in the United States of America

7032018

To Richard,
my brother

IN PRAISE OF GOD THE CREATOR

The World Around Us

IN PRAISE OF GOD THE REDEEMER

The Kingdom Within

Let everything that hath breath praise the Lord.

Because you are alive, you can respond!
Praise is response,
the voluntary response
of our total selves
or even a part of ourselves
to the presence and doings of the Lord,
Creator-Redeemer-God.
Praise is the astonishment we express
when touched by his infinity,
by his intimacy,
by his attention concentrated on each one of us.
Praise is the silence of awe we feel
when we recognize a miracle,
the wholeness we feel
in the arms of Almighty Love,
the freedom we know,
once captured, changed, kindled.
Let us respond
to the One
in whom we live
and move
and have our being.
Let us praise the Lord.

Joyce Blackburn

M. Bentley

In Praise
of God
the Creator

The World Around Us

In Praise of Beginnings

You know, Lord, how many things I begin.
You know how many go unfinished.
At times my life seems to be a tangle of loose
    ends.
What you begin
you complete,
even while you continue creating.
How you can finish and continue at the same
    time
is beyond me.
But I know you are doing it
in us and in our world.
I have learned that you cannot stall,
turn stale, become static,
because you are ever in motion toward us
even though you cannot change.
Truly, that is beyond me!
Source of beginnings,
this difference between your nature and mine
evokes my worship and my praise.

Joyce Blackburn

Before all time, before all worlds,
Before the dawn of every age, the dawn of every
    world,
Is God! And He remains
Beyond all coming ages, and beyond
All unthought worlds that yet may be!

Namdev

In the beginning you laid the foundations of
    the earth,
    and the heavens are the work of your hands.
They will perish, but you remain;
    they will all wear out like a garment.
Like clothing you will change them
    and they will be discarded.
But you remain the same,
    and your years will never end.

Psalm 102:25–27 NIV

For since the creation of the world his invisible
attributes—his everlasting power and
divinity—are to be discerned and contemplated
in his works.

Romans 1:20

He who does not praise God while here on earth
shall in eternity be dumb.

John of Ruysbroeck

THE CREATION

And God stepped out on space,
And he looked around and said:
I'm lonely—
I'll make me a world.

And far as the eye of God could see
Darkness covered everything,
Blacker than a hundred midnights
Down in a cypress swamp.

Then God smiled,
And the light broke,
And the darkness rolled up on one side,
And the light stood shining on the other,
And God said: That's good!

Then God reached out and took the light in his
    hands,
And God rolled the light around in his hands
Until he made the sun;
And he set that sun a-blazing in the heavens.
And the light that was left from making the sun
God gathered it up in a shining ball
And flung it against the darkness,
Spangling the night with the moon and stars.
Then down between
The darkness and the light
He hurled the world;
And God said: That's good!

Then God himself stepped down—
And the sun was on his right hand,
And the moon was on his left;
The stars were clustered about his head,
And the earth was under his feet.
And God walked, and where he trod
His footsteps hollowed the valleys out
And bulged the mountains up.

Then he stopped and looked and saw
That the earth was hot and barren.
So God stepped over to the edge of the world
And he spat out the seven seas—
He batted his eyes, and the lightnings flashed—
He clapped his hands, and the thunders rolled—
And the waters above the earth came down,
The cooling waters came down.

Then the green grass sprouted,
And the little red flowers blossomed,
The pine tree pointed his finger to the sky,
And the oak spread out his arms,
The lakes cuddled down in the hollows of the
    ground,
And the rivers ran down to the sea;
And God smiled again,
And the rainbow appeared,
And curled itself around his shoulder.

Then God raised his arm and he waved his hand
Over the sea and over the land,
And he said: Bring forth! Bring forth!
And quicker than God could drop his hand,
Fishes and fowls
And beasts and birds
Swam the rivers and the seas,
Roamed the forests and the woods,
And split the air with their wings.
And God said: That's good!

Then God walked around,
And God looked around
On all that he had made.
He looked at his sun,
And he looked at his moon,
And he looked at his little stars;
He looked on his world
With all its living things,
And God said: I'm lonely still.

Then God sat down—
On the side of a hill where he could think;
By a deep, wide river he sat down;
With his head in his hands,
God thought and thought,
Till he thought: I'll make me a man!

Up from the bed of the river
God scooped the clay;
And by the bank of the river
He kneeled him down;
And there the great God Almighty
Who lit the sun and fixed it in the sky,
Who flung the stars to the most far corner of the
    night,
Who rounded the earth in the middle of his hand;
This Great God,
Like a mammy bending over her baby,
Kneeled down in the dust
Toiling over a lump of clay
Till he shaped it in his own image;

Then into it he blew the breath of life,
And man became a living soul.
Amen. Amen.

James Weldon Johnson

God creates out of *nothing*. Wonderful, you say.
Yes, to be sure, but He does what is still more
wonderful: He makes saints out of sinners.

Soren Kierkegaard

For if there is an infinitely wise and good Creator, in whom we live, move, and have our being, whose providence governs all things in all places, surely it must be the highest act of our understanding to conceive rightly of Him; it must be the noblest instance of judgment, the most exalted temper of our nature, to worship and adore this universal providence, to conform to its laws, to study its wisdom, and to live and act everywhere, as in the presence of this infinitely good and wise Creator.

William Law

By means of all created things, without exception, the divine assails us, penetrates us and moulds us. We imagined it as distant and inaccessible, whereas in fact we live steeped in its burning layers. . . .

The world, this palpable world, to which we brought the boredom and callousness reserved for profane places, is in truth a holy place, and we did not know it. *Venite, adoremus.*

Pierre Teilhard de Chardin

Praise the LORD, O my soul.

O LORD my God, you are very great;
    you are clothed with splendor and majesty.
He wraps himself in light as with a garment;
    he stretches out the heavens like a tent
    and lays the beams of his upper chambers
        on their waters.
He makes the clouds his chariot
    and rides on the wings of the wind.
He makes winds his messengers,
    flames of fire his servants.

He set the earth on its foundations;
    it can never be moved.
You covered it with the deep as with a garment;
    the waters stood above the mountains.
But at your rebuke the waters fled,
    at the sound of your thunder they took to
        flight;
they flowed over the mountains,
    they went down into the valleys,
    to the place you assigned for them.
You set a boundary they cannot cross;
    never again will they cover the earth.

He makes springs pour water into the ravines;
    it flows between the mountains.
They give water to all the beasts of the field;
    the wild donkeys quench their thirst.
The birds of the air nest by the waters;
    they sing among the branches.
He waters the mountains from his upper
        chambers;
    the earth is satisfied by the fruit of his work.
He makes grass grow for the cattle,
    and plants for man to cultivate—
    bringing forth food from the earth:
wine that gladdens the heart of man,
    oil to make his face shine,
    and bread that sustains his heart.

The trees of the LORD are well watered,
  the cedars of Lebanon that he planted.
There the birds make their nests;
  the stork has its home in the pine trees.
The high mountains belong to the wild goats;
  the crags are a refuge for the coneys.

The moon marks off the seasons,
  and the sun knows when to go down.
You bring darkness, it becomes night,
  and all the beasts of the forest prowl.
The lions roar for their prey
  and seek their food from God.
The sun rises, and they steal away;
  they return and lie down in their dens.
Then man goes out to his work,
  to his labor until evening.

How many are your works, O Lord!
  In wisdom you made them all;
  the earth is full of your creatures.

Psalm 104 NIV

Praise ye the Lord, His mighty works acclaim;
His years are endless, Yet is He the same.
O sing His praise, Give glory to His holy name.
Alleluia. Alleluia. Amen.

Duncan Howlett

Rise, O my soul, with thy desires to heaven,
And with divinest contemplation use thy time.

To worship is to quicken the conscience by the holiness of God, to feed the mind with the truth of God, to open the heart to the love of God, to devote the will to the purpose of God. All this is gathered up in that emotion which most cleanses us from selfishness because it is the most selfless of all emotions—adoration.

William Temple

The truth of a thing is the blossom of it, the thing it is made for. Truth in a man's imagination is the power to recognize this truth of a thing; and wherever, in anything that God has made, in the glory of it, be it sky or flower or human face, we see the glory of God, there a true imagination is beholding a truth of God.

George MacDonald

PARAPHRASE ON PSALM 67

May we continually be the recipients of God's
    mercy and blessing
In order that we may demonstrate His order and
    purpose throughout the earth
And His redemptive power to the creatures of this
    world.

And may it ultimately resolve in all of God's sons
Lifting their voices in praise to their Lord and
    God.

The nations of the earth would truly abide in
    peace and sing for joy
If they would allow God to be their God
And if they would direct their destinies according
    to His will.

Then the inhabitants of this world would surely lift
    their voices in praise to their Lord and God.

The earth continues to receive the abundance of
    God.
His blessings are all about us.

May every mountain and valley, plain and forest,
May every city street with its teeming apartments
    and sprawling suburbs
Echo with the praises of men to their God.

Leslie F. Brandt

In Praise of Observations

In spite of my neglect,
destruction, waste,
the world around me
reveals beauty and order still.
The sun, for example,
does not fail;
taken for granted
because on time.
I cannot watch it rise
without a sense of wonder,
wonder planted in my childhood,
lasting a lifetime,
"an unfailing antidote,"
Rachel Carson called it,
"antidote against boredom
and disenchantment,
the sterile preoccupation
with things artificial."
A sense of wonder
rooted in elements
and mysterious life:
The sun,
its mirror-moon,
other stars,
the land and sea,
water and sky,
swimming, roving, flying creatures,
plants and seeds,
male and female,
natural to my habitat,
clues to the world which was meant to be.

Joyce Blackburn

Sunrise: hidden by pines and cedars to the east: I saw the red flame of the kingly sun glaring through the black trees, not like dawn but like a forest fire. Then the sun became distinguished as a person and he shone silently and with solemn power through the branches, and the whole world was silent and calm.

Sunrise is an event that calls forth solemn music in the very depths of man's nature, as if one's whole being had to attune itself to the cosmos and praise God for the new day, praise Him in the name of all the creatures that ever were or ever will be. I look at the rising sun and feel that now upon me falls the responsibility of seeing what all my ancestors have seen . . . praising God before me. Whether or not they praised Him then, for themselves, they must praise Him now in me. When the sun rises each one of us is summoned by the living and the dead to praise God.

Thomas Merton

I feel that a man may be happy in this world and I know that this world is a world of imagination and vision. I see everything I paint in this world but everybody does not see alike. To the eye of a miser a guinea is far more beautiful than the sun and a bag worn with the use of money has more beautiful proportions than a vine filled with grapes. The tree which moves some to tears of joy is in the eyes of others only a green thing which stands in the way. As a man is so he sees.

When the sun rises, do you not see a round disk of fire something like a gold piece? O no, no, I see an innumerable company of the heavenly host crying "Holy, Holy, Holy, is the Lord God Almighty." I do not question my bodily eye any more than I would question a window concerning sight. I look through it and not with it.

William Blake

Many and great, O God, are thy things,
Maker of earth and sky;
Thy hands have set the heavens with stars;
Thy fingers spread the mountains and plains.
Lo, at thy word the waters were formed;
Deep seas obey thy voice.

Grant unto us communion with thee,
Thou star-abiding one;
Come unto us and dwell with us;
With thee are found the gifts of life.
Bless us with life that has no end,
Eternal life with thee. Amen.

American Folk Hymn
Paraphrase by Philip Frazier

The Spirit of God was hovering over the waters. . . . And God said, "Let there be an expanse between the waters to separate water from water."

Genesis 1:1, 6 NIV

God made sun and moon to distinguish seasons, and day and night, and we cannot have the fruits of the earth but in their seasons: but God hath made no decree to distinguish the seasons of his mercies; in paradise the fruits were ripe the first minute, and in heaven it is always autumn, his mercies are ever in their maturity. We ask *panem quotidianum,* our daily bread, and God never says you should have come yesterday, he never says you must come again tomorrow, but "today if you will hear his voice," today he will hear you. If some king of the earth hath so large an extent of dominion in north and south, as that he hath winter and summer together in his dominions, so large an extent east and west, as that he hath day and night together in his dominions, much more hath God mercy and judgment together: . . . though . . . thou have been benighted till now, wintred and frozen, clouded and eclipsed, damped and benumbed, smothered and stupified till now, how God comes to thee, not as in the dawning of the day, not as in the bud of the spring, but as the sun at noon to illustrate all shadows, as the sheaves in harvest, to fill all penuries, all occasions invite his mercies, and all times are his seasons.

John Donne

GOD OF THE NEBULAE

Lover of all, I hold me fast by Thee,
Ruler of time, King of eternity
There is no great with Thee, there is no small,
For Thou art all, and fillest all in all.

The new-born world swings forth at Thy
    command,
The falling dewdrop falls into Thy hand.
God of the firmament's mysterious powers,
I see Thee thread the minutes of my hours.

I see Thee guide the frail, the fading moon
That walks alone through empty skies at noon.
Was ever way-worn, lonely traveller
But had Thee by him, blessèd Comforter?

Out of my vision swims the untracked star,
Thy counsels too are high and very far,
Only I know, God of the nebulae,
It is enough to hold me fast by Thee.

Amy Carmichael

Every evening that the sun sets; every night
that the moon conquers the deep blue darkness
of the starry heavens; every morning that the
morning star rises to herald the coming of the
sun; every new day that is born out of night; the
whole coming and going of light; and in a very
special way the waning moon, which eventually
becomes just the white-grey ash of the faintly
gleaming new moon and yet rises again and
becomes once more the radiant full moon—all
this points to the mystery of the marvelous victory
won by light over darkness, by good over evil.

Eberhard Arnold

When I heard the learn'd astronomer,
When the proofs, the figures, were ranged in columns before me,
When I was shown the charts and diagrams, to add, divide, and measure them,
When I was sitting heard the astronomer when he lectured with much applause in the lecture-room,
How soon unaccountable I became tired and sick,
Till rising and gliding out I wander'd off by myself,
In the mystical moist night-air, and from time to time,
Look'd up in perfect silence at the stars.

Walt Whitman

So far, no planet in our solar system has proved to have surface water as ours has. Liquid water, that is. Vapors and ice may be on others, but when you look at photographs of earth from space, you see a blue globe out there in the black emptiness. Clouds wrap it, yes, but the whole planet looks as though it were covered by water. *Aquarius.* Water makes the environment of earth unique, and everything here depends upon it. You may know that a tomato is 95 percent water, but did you know that human blood is 83 percent water? "It is an interesting biological fact," wrote John F. Kennedy, "that all of us have in our veins the exact same percentage of salt in our blood that exists in the ocean. . . . We have salt in our blood, in our sweat, in our tears."

Joyce Blackburn

In Praise of Mysteries and Molecules

The natural universe
may never give up all of its secrets.
Countless experiments,
discoveries and probes,
surfeit of data
too vast to compute
could choke us first.
Best to recall that long before
I could explain a conch shell—
that whorl of carbonate of calcium—
the child-me could imagine
the roar of the sea
by holding a conch to my ear.
Experiencing that mystery
made a timeless memory.
Explanations are more likely
to be filed, outdated—and forgotten?

Joyce Blackburn

In one salutation to thee, my God, let all my senses spread out and touch this world at thy feet.

Like a rain-cloud of July hung low with its burden of unshed showers, let all my mind bend down at thy door in one salutation to thee.

Let all my songs gather together their diverse strains into a single current and flow to a sea of silence in one salutation to thee.

Like a flock of homesick cranes flying night and day back to their mountain nests, let all my life take its voyage to its eternal home in one salutation to thee.

Rabindranath Tagore

When I touch that flower,
I am touching infinity.
I learn what I know
by watching and loving
everything.

George Washington Carver

The most beautiful thing we can experience is the mystery.

Albert Einstein

This world, as a glorious apartment of the boundless palace of the sovereign Creator, is furnished with an infinite variety of animated scenes, inexpressibly beautiful and pleasing, equally free to the inspection and enjoyment of all his creatures.

William Bartram

NATURE'S PRESCRIPTIONS

1

Once the dew has fallen,
walk barefooted in the grass
if you want to sleep well.

2

If you can't afford a carpet,
walk barefooted on the moss
in the woods. You will feel rich.

3

Walking in your bare feet
on a sandy beach is better
than taking nerve tonic.

4

Walking in snow
rejuvenates the appetite.
But you'd best
keep your boots on.

Joyce Blackburn

Both Job and Thoreau were familiar with the
mysteries—

Hast thou entered into the treasures of the snow? or hast thou seen the treasures of the hail? . . . By what way is the light parted, which scattereth the east wind upon the earth? Who hath divided a watercourse for the overflowing of waters, or a way for the lightning of thunder; to cause it to rain on the earth, where no man is; on the wilderness, wherein there is no man; to satisfy the desolate and waste ground; and to cause the bud of the tender herb to spring forth? Hath the rain a father? or who hath begotten the drops of dew? Out of whose womb came the ice? and the hoary frost of heaven, who hath engendered it? . . . Canst thou bind the sweet influences of Pleiades, or loose the bands of Orion? . . . Canst thou send lightnings, that they may go, and say unto thee, Here we are?

Job 38:22–35 KJV

I wish to forget, a considerable part of every day, all mean, narrow, trivial men. . . and therefore I come out to these solitudes, where the problem of existence is simplified. I get away a mile or two from the town into the stillness and solitude of nature, with rocks, trees, weeds, snow about me. I enter some glade in the woods, perchance, where a few weeds and dry leaves alone lift themselves above the surface of the snow, and it is as if I had come to an open window. I see out and around myself. . . . This stillness, solitude, wildness of nature is a kind of thoroughwort, or boneset, to my intellect. This is what I go out to seek. It is as if I always met in those places some grand, serene, immortal, infinitely encouraging, though invisible, companion, and walked with him.

Henry David Thoreau

O ye frost and cold,
O ye ice and snow,
bless ye the Lord,
praise Him and magnify Him
forever.

Joyce Blackburn

*There is a legend which claims that if you eat
of the snowberry, you will become
all-knowing about flowers. Henry Van Dyke,
who believed it, wrote,*

You will know where to find the yellow violet,
and the wake-robin, and the pink lady-slipper,
and the scarlet sage, and the fringed gentian. You
will understand how the buds trust themselves
to the spring in their unfolding, and how the
blossoms trust themselves to the winter in their
withering, and how the busy hands of Nature are
ever weaving the beautiful garment of life out
of the strands of death, and nothing is lost that
yields itself to her quiet handling.

Beyond the world of outward perception there
is another world of inward vision, and the key to it
is imagination. To see things as they are—that is
a precious gift. To see things as they were in their
beginning, or as they will be in their ending, or as
they ought to be in their perfecting; to make the
absent, present; to rebuild the past out of a
fragment of carven stone; to foresee the future
harvest in the grain of wheat in the sower's hand;
to visualize the face of the invisible, and enter into
the lives of all sorts and conditions of unknown
men—that is a far more precious gift.

Henry Van Dyke

And journeying on . . . St. Francis lifted up his eyes and beheld some trees by the wayside whereon were an infinite number of birds; so that he marvelled and said to his companions, "Tarry here for me by the way and I will go and preach to my little sisters the birds." And he entered into a field and began to preach to the birds that were on the ground; and anon those that were on the trees flew down to hear him, and all stood still the while St. Francis made an end of his sermon; and even then they departed not until he had given them his blessing. . . .

And the substance of the sermon St. Francis preached was this: "My little sisters the birds, much are ye beholden to God your Creator, and always and in every place ye ought to praise Him for that He hath given you—double and—triple vesture; He hath given you freedom to go into every place and also did preserve the seed of you in the ark of Noah, in order that your kind might not perish from the earth. Again, ye are beholden to him for the element of air which he hath appointed for you; moreover ye sow not, neither do ye reap, and God feedeth you and giveth you the rivers and the fountains for your drink; He giveth you the mountains and valleys for your refuge, and the tall trees wherein to build your nests, and forasmuch as ye can neither spin nor sew God clotheth you, you and your children: wherefore your Creator loveth you much, since He hath dealt so bounteously with you; and therefore beware little sisters mine, of the sin of ingratitude, but ever strive to praise God."

While St. Francis was uttering these words, all those birds began to open their beaks, and stretch their necks, and spread their wings and reverently to bow their heads to the ground, showing by their gestures and songs that the holy father's words gave them greatest joy: and St. Francis was glad and rejoiced with them, and marvelled much at so great a multitude of birds and at their manifold loveliness, and at their attention and familiarity, for which things he devoutly praised the Creator in them.

The Little Flowers of St. Francis

St. Francis must have been a bird watcher! Noah was. He sent a dove from the ark to bring back proof that flood waters were receding. To locate strange, distant, invisible coasts, the ancient Vikings took along birds on their exploratory trips. Today, the most sophisticated watchers are scientists who are trying to figure out the forecasting, navigational, and endurance secrets of birds. They have learned already that birds can forecast weather and seasons, detect barometric pressure change, navigate by the sun, navigate by stars, navigate by earth's magnetic field, see light and respond to sound, migrate by a biological clock so accurate in some cases, they return in spring on the same day to the same limb on the same tree. They attain astounding speed:

> small species—30 m.p.h.
> geese—60 m.p.h.
> peregrines—180 m.p.h.

Birds exhibit phenomenal stamina. For example, the arctic tern can fly many thousands of miles from the Arctic to the Antarctic regions.

Does the hawk take flight by your wisdom
   and spread his wings toward the south?
Does the eagle soar at your command
   and build his nest on high?

Even the stork in the sky
   knows her appointed seasons,
and the dove, the swift and the thrush
   observe the time of their migration.

Job 39:26–27; Jeremiah 8:7 NIV

GETTING INSIDE THE MIRACLE

No, He is too quick. We never
catch Him at it. He is there
sooner than our thought or prayer.
Searching
backward, we cannot discover *how*
or get inside the miracle.

Even if it were here and now
how would we describe the just-born trees
swimming into place at their green creation,
flowering upward in the air
with all their thin twigs quivering
in the gusts of grace? or the great
white whales fluking
through crystalline seas
like recently-inflated balloons? Who could time
the beat of the man's heart
as the woman comes close enough to fill
his newly-hollow side? Who will
diagram the gynecology
of incarnation, the trigonometry of trinity?
or chemically analyze wine
from a well? or see inside
joints as they loosen, and whole limbs
and lives? Will anyone stand beside
the moving stone? and plot the bright
trajectory of the ascension? and explain
the tongues of fire
telling both heat and light?

Enough. Refrain.
Observe a finished work. Think:
Today—another miracle—the feathered
arrows of my faith may link
God's bow and target.

Luci Shaw

In Praise of Color, Especially Green

"Of all stones, the emerald is the most
    precious . . .
'Green sings!' . . .
Machinery cannot be used to mine emeralds . . .
emeralds are picked tediously by hand,
from the sharp washed broken rocks
which form their 'pockets' . . .
When first taken from their greenish quartz
    'pockets'
where they are formed, emeralds are very fragile
and must be 'toughened' by exposure
to the air for some time . . .
Gem-cutters in ancient times
kept an emerald near-by
to rest their eyes.
Green is a singing color.
It is also a restful color. . . ."
Amazing facts found in a book of meditations.*
The fact which cannot be proven
is that green sings. But you can hear it.

*Eugenia Price, *Share My Pleasant Stones* (Zondervan
1967)

O most high, almighty, good Lord God, to Thee belong praise, glory, honour, and all blessing!

Praised be my Lord God with all His creatures; and specially our brother the sun, who brings us the day, and who brings us the light; fair is he, and shining with a very great splendour: O Lord, to us he signifies Thee!

Praised be my Lord for our sister the moon, and for the stars, the which He has set clear and lovely in heaven.

Praised be my Lord for our brother the wind, and for air and cloud, calms and all weather, by the which Thou upholdest in life all creatures.

Praised be my Lord for our sister water, who is very serviceable unto us, and humble, and precious, and clean.

Praised be my Lord for our brother fire, through whom Thou givest us light in the darkness; and he is bright, and pleasant, and very mighty, and strong.

Praised be my Lord for our mother the earth, the which doth sustain and keep us, and bringeth forth divers fruits, and flowers of many colours, and grass. . . .

Praise ye, and bless ye the Lord, and give thanks unto Him, and serve Him with great humility.

St. Francis

When the green woods laugh with the voice of
    joy,
And the dimpling stream runs laughing by;
When the air does laugh with our merry wit,
And the green hill laughs with the noise of it;
When the meadow laughs with lively green,
And the grasshopper laughs in the merry scene,
When Mary and Susan and Emily
With their sweet round mouths sing "Ha, ha, he!"
When the painted birds laugh in the shade,
When our table with cherries and nuts is spread,
Come live, and be merry, and join with me,
To sing the sweet chorus of "Ha, ha, he!"

William Blake

GREEN BLACKBOARDS

The school is up-to-date.
Proudly the principal enumerates all the
      improvements.
The finest discovery, Lord, is the green
      blackboards.
The scientists have studied the matter at length,
    they have made experiments;
We now know that green is the ideal color, that
      it doesn't tire the eyes, that it is quieting
      and relaxing.

It has occurred to me, Lord, that you didn't
      wait so long to paint the trees and the
      meadows green.
Your research laboratories were efficient, and
      in order not to tire us, you perfected a
      number of shades of green for your
      modern meadows.
And so the "finds" of men consist in
      discovering what you have thought
      from time immemorial.
Thank you, Lord, for being the good Father
      who gives his children the joy of
      discovering by themselves the
      treasures of his intelligence and love.
But keep us from believing that by ourselves we
      have invented anything at all.

Michel Quoist

It is very easy, when talking about creation, to conceive of God's part in it as simply getting the ball rolling—as if he were a kind of divine billiard cue, after whose action inexorable laws took over and excused him from further involvement with the balls, But that won't work. This world is *fundamentally* unnecessary. Nothing *has* to be. It needs a creator, not only for its beginning, but for every moment of its being. Accordingly, the Trinitarian bash doesn't really come *before* creation; what actually happens is that all of creation, from start to finish, occurs within the bash—that the raucousness of the divine party is simultaneous with the being of everything that ever was or will be. If you like paradoxes, it means that God is the eternal contemporary of all the events and beings in time.

Which is where the refinement in the analogy comes in. What happens is not that the Trinity manufactures the first duck and then the ducks take over the duck business as a kind of cottage industry. It is that every duck, down at the roots of its being, at the level where what is needed is not the ability to fertilize duck eggs, but the moxie to stand outside of nothing—to *be* when there is no necessity of being—every duck, at that level, is a response to the creative act of God. In terms of the analogy, it means that God the Father *thinks up* duck #47307 for the month of May, A.D. . . . , that God the Spirit rushes over to the edge of the formless void and, with unutterable groaning, *broods* duck #47307, and that over his brooding God the Son, the eternal Word, triumphantly *shouts,* "Duck #47307!" And presto! you have a duck. Not one, you will note, tossed off in response to some mindless decree that there may as well be ducks as alligators, but one neatly fielded up in a game of delight by the eternal archetypes of Tinker, Evers and Chance. The world is not God's surplus inventory of artifacts; it is a whole barrelful of the apples of his eye, constantly juggled, relished and exchanged by the persons of the Trinity.

R. F. Capon

Create in me a clean heart, O God;
and renew a right spirit within me.

Psalm 51:10 KJV

Is creation a word which happened once,
And it was done,
Or does God continue to create?
   Is created life a set pattern
   Which is passed blindly from generation to
      generation,
     Or does it change in the passing
     So that even as it goes it changes form
     And creates new ways of being?

Creation . . .
God, who created,
May continue to create.
   And if I stand still, unchanging,
   I may find myself out of the flow
   Of that creation.

Gordon and Gladis DePree

Below the north pasture the creek water is a strange, evil, salamander green. Its winding snake course is marked by the winking silver bubbles. Right . . . left . . . right . . . left . . . spiraling down to the river, carrying its load of waste to the sea. Lift the green algae with a stick and they come up in heavy green nets and veils.

The gnats dance in front of my eyes. They use my eyeballs for a mirror and dance for their own delectation. They do not light, but they drive me crazy. Twigs crack in the wilderness of green, but nothing comes.

The maidenflies open four black velvet wings. The dragonflies of this pool are black and milky blue. The stream flows over beautiful stones, past green thickets of horsetail plants, a miniature forest of fir trees. The only sound is the crisp-paper crackling of the dragonfly wings, and then a kingfisher rattles. I sit very still. Something seems to be coming up the creek. A soft sound. Then I feel the wind. It blows the gnats away. It sways the stems, and the bodies of maidenflies—the electric-blue bodies, the turquoise green. The coming of a breeze on a still, hot day is an awesome, lovely thing. *One finds oneself praising God against one's will. The relief!*

Josephine W. Johnson

But what do I love when I love Thee? Not grace of bodies, nor the beauty of the seasons, nor the brightness of the light . . . nor inexhaustible melodies of sweet song, nor the fragrant smell of flowers, of ointments and spices. . . . None of these love I when I love my God: and yet I love a kind of light, and of melody and of fragrance . . . when I love my God. . . .

And what is this? I asked the earth and it said, "I am not He," and whatsoever is in it confessed the same. I asked the sea and the deeps, and all that swimming or creeping live therein, and they answered, "We are not thy God, seek above us." I asked the wandering winds; and the whole air with his inhabitants spoke, "I am not God." I asked the heavens, sun, moon and stars, "Nor (say they) are we the God whom thou seekest." And I replied unto all those things which encompass the door of my flesh, "Ye have told me of my God, that ye are not He: tell me something of Him." And they cried all with a great voice, "He made us." My questioning them was my mind's desire, and their Beauty was their answer.

St. Augustine

"I give her six months," said a hopeful medical. But I had thought my call was for life. To add to the depression of the hour there was the flatness that comes after fever; and the doubtless true but rather melancholy lines . . . sighed themselves over monotonously.

Thou shalt need all the strength that God can give.

Simply to live, my friend, simply to live.

. Then suddenly like the blue flash of a kingfisher's wing, like the quick flight of a flock of little birds, these words came flying through the wood: *"I have as much grace for you as I have green for My trees."* And I knew that our Father had spoken to me as one might speak to a child.

The green of millions of trees, fold upon fold of green velvet spread upon the mountains, vast and limitless like the seas. . . . It was an inexhaustible word.

O Jesus, Lover of Thy least lovable, most foolish, least useful little child, we Thy little children thank Thee. Thou hast as much grace for us as Thou hast green for Thy trees, grace to help in time of need. Thou canst make something of the least of us. Thou canst make us to be "Life, fire, wing, force."

Amy Carmichael

I was utterly alone with the sun and the earth. Lying down on the grass, I spoke in my soul to the earth, the sun, the air, and the distant sea far beyond sight. I thought of the earth's firmness—I felt it bear me up; through the grassy couch there came an influence as if I could feel the great earth speaking to me. I thought of the wandering air—its pureness, which is its beauty; the air touched me and gave me something of itself. I spoke to the sea: though so far, in my mind I saw it, green at the rim of the earth and blue in deeper ocean. . . . I turned to the blue heaven over, gazing into its depth, inhaling its exquisite colour and sweetness. The rich blue of the unattainable flower of the sky drew my soul towards it, and there it rested, for *pure colour is rest of heart.* By all these I prayed. . . . Then, returning, I prayed by the sweet thyme, whose little flowers I touched with my hand; by the slender grass; by the crumble of dry chalky earth I took up and let fall through my fingers. Touching the crumble of earth, the blade of grass, the thyme flower, breathing the earth-encircling air, thinking of the sea and the sky, holding out my hand for the sunbeams to touch it, prone on the sward in token of deep reverence, thus I prayed.

Richard Jefferies

MAY 20: VERY EARLY MORNING

all the field praises Him/all
dandelions are his glory/gold
and silver/all trilliums unfold
white flames above their trinities
of leaves all wild strawberries
and massed woods violets reflect His skies'
clean blue and white
all brambles/all oxeyes
all stalks and stems lift . . . .

. . . . s

carnon touch/last year's yarrow (raising
brittle star skeletons) tells
age is not past praising
all small low unknown
unnamed weeds show His impossible greens
all grasses sing
tone on clear tone
all mosses spread a spring-
soft velvet for His feet
and by all means
all leaves/buds/all flowers cup
jewels of fire and ice
holding up
to His kind morning heat
a silver sacrifice

now
make of our hearts a field
to raise Your praise

Luci Shaw

In Praise

As ancient as our race
is the urge to sing,
to perform on instruments.
Why, who knows how old
cymbals may be?
David called for cymbals
loud-sounding, clanging!
Without dispute, he was
"a musician of some reputation."
I wonder if his melodies
matched the lyrics he wrote.
If so, I cannot doubt
he cured Saul's psychosis!
How often do you read a psalm
for healing?
How often do you frame your joy,
your adoration
in David's stanzas?
He is the one who said Sing,
"Let everything that hath breath. . . ."
All together now!

Joyce Blackburn

For there is nothing that so clears a way for your prayers, nothing that so disperses dullness of heart, nothing that so purifies the soul from poor and little passions, nothing that so opens heaven, or carries your heart so near it, as these songs of praise.

They create a sense and delight in God, they awaken holy desires, they teach you how to ask, and they prevail with God to give. They kindle a holy flame, they turn your heart into an altar, your prayers into incense, and carry them as a sweet-smelling savour to the throne of grace.

William Lau

Is any among you afflicted? Let him pray.
Is any merry? let him sing psalms.

James 5:13

Sing joyfully to the Lord, you righteous;
*   it is fitting for the upright to praise him.*
Praise the Lord with the harp;
*   make music to him on the ten-stringed lyre.*
Sing to him a new song;
*   play skillfully, and shout for joy.*

Psalm 33:1–3 NIV

All people that on earth do dwell,
Sing to the Lord with cheerful voice.
Him serve with mirth, his praise forth tell;
Come ye before him and rejoice.
Know that the Lord is God indeed;
Without our aid he did us make;
We are his folk, he doth us feed,
And for his sheep he doth us take.
O enter then his gates with praise,
Approach with joy his courts unto;
Praise, laud, and bless his name always,
For it is seemly so to do.
For why! the Lord our God is good;
His mercy is forever sure;
His truth at all times firmly stood,
And shall from age to age endure.

Psalm 100
William Kethe

That day I felt like Jonah inside the whale. There was not one bit of good news anywhere on the planet. And my small piece of the world was falling to pieces. When the telephone rang, I knew a special friend was not "doing so well" in the hospital.

My past failures clogged my throat like smog. Living was a dead-end street.

I was sitting by the big window with my hands over my aching eyes. Suddenly a strange sound from outside made me open them. The sound came from the boat landing on the bank of Mill Pond. I opened the front door, and I could see a small dark silhouette on the shingle. The sound came clearly now across the shining blue water. It was clean, poignant, penetrating, and mournful. Still it was thrilling. As I watched, the figure turned, and I knew it was a man playing bagpipes. Bagpipes here on a quiet Cape Cod shore framed by pine woods?

Only the bagpiper and I seemed to be in the landscape.

Yet, we were not alone. Three seagulls patterned the luminous sky with their wings. Then the hawk who lives in the cedar near my house mounted his drift of air and swooped across the water. What had he seen? I wondered what small quivering prey was hiding in the beach grasses or the sea lavender?

The bagpipes wailed on. Then, from the little duck pond leading to the big expanse came seven of the Canada geese, majestically swimming toward their breakfast minnows. (Schools of fish mark their location by a glassy area on the surface.) The mate of the seventh goose was not there. She swam alone. I looked about for him. He might still be along; the little duck pond just below my windows is a secluded wildlife haven. The geese will fly south soon; they are already arguing about it. Their strong clarion tones made an accompaniment to the skirling of the lonely bagpipe.

Interested now, I went out just as a flaming cardinal dropped to the birdbath and began thrashing about in the cold water.

Tiny Tim, the red squirrel, bounced along the split rail fence and onto the roof of the bird feeder where his orange halves were nailed. As I turned to go back into the house, I just missed stepping on the wee toad who lives in the petunia border where the outside faucet drips. No bigger than a thumbnail, he can still hop to the brick doorstep. He is not at all afraid. He dozes in the morning sun. Fragile as a leaf, his little body is perfectly equipped for survival in a giant world.

The music of the bagpipe rose into a deep round melody, some old Scottish marching song. Then it faded away as the player walked up to the road and vanished.

Inside the house, I went to my workroom and sat down at the typewriter, my kitten skimming after me. I rolled the paper in the machine.

I began to sing, and I was singing my favorite hymn, "Amazing Grace."

Gladys Taber

THE SINGERS

God sent his singers upon earth
With songs of sadness and of mirth,
That they might touch the hearts of men,
And bring them back to heaven again.

The first a youth, with soul of fire
Held in his hand a golden lyre;
Through groves he wandered, and by streams,
Playing the music of our dreams.

The second, with a bearded face,
Stood singing in the market-place,
And stirred with accents deep and loud
The hearts of all the listening crowd.

A gray, old man, the third and last,
Sang in cathedrals dim and vast
While the majestic organ rolled
Contrition from its mouths of gold.

And those who heard the Singers three
Disputed which the best might be;
For still the music seemed to start
Discordant echoes in each heart.

But the great Master said, "I see
No best in kind, but in degree;
I gave a various gift to each,
To charm, to strengthen, and to teach.

"These are the three great chords of might,
And he whose ear is tuned aright
Will hear no discord in the three,
But the most perfect harmony."

Henry Wadsworth Longfellow

Pure music, quite apart from all other conceptions of the imagination, touches the nerves and all organs of hearing and thus changes our inner feelings. . . . The entire being begins to resound. . . . Our feeling is nothing but an inner music, a constant oscillation of the vital nerves. Everything that surrounds us, all our new ideas and sensations increase or diminish, strengthen or weaken the state of these inner oscillations. Music touches the nerves in a peculiar manner and results in a singular playfulness, a quite special communication that cannot be described in words. Music represents the inner feeling in the exterior air, and expresses what precedes, accompanies, or follows all verbal utterance.

Wilhelm Heinse

Music is being played to the cows in the milking barn. Rules have been made and confirmed: only sacred music is to be played to the cows, not "classical" music. The music is to make the cows give more milk. The sacred music is to keep the brothers who work in the cow barn recollected. For some time now sacred music has been played to the cows in the milking barn. They have not given more milk. The brothers have not been any more recollected than usual. I believe the cows will soon be hearing Beethoven. Then we shall have classical, perhaps worldly milk and the monastery will prosper. (Later: It was true. The hills resounded with Beethoven. The monastery has prospered. The brother mainly concerned with the music, however, departed.)

Thomas Merton

Figured bass is the most perfect foundation of music. It is executed with both hands in such a manner that the left hand plays the notes that are written, while the right adds consonances and dissonances thereto, making an agreeable harmony for the glory of God and the justifiable gratification of the soul. Like all music, the figured bass should have no other end and aim than the glory of God and the recreation of the soul; where this is not kept in mind there is no true music, but only an infernal clamour and ranting.

Johann Sebastian Bach

Music must serve a purpose; it must be a part of something larger than itself, a part of humanity, and that, indeed, is at the core of my argument with music of today—its lack of humanity. A musician is also a man, and more important than his music is his attitude toward life. Nor can the two be separated.

Each day I am reborn. All my life I have started each day in the same manner. It is not a mechanical routine, but something essential to my daily life. First I go to nature; it is a rediscovery of the world of which I have the joy of being a part. It fills me with the awareness of the wonder of life, with a feeling of incredible marvel of being a human being. Then, I go to the piano and I play two Preludes and Fugues of Bach. It is a sort of benediction on the house. The music is never the same for me, each day is something new, fantastic and unbelievable. That is Bach, like nature, a miracle.

Pablo Casals

*And be not drunk with wine, wherein is excess;
but be filled with the Spirit; Speaking to
yourselves in psalms and hymns and spiritual
songs, singing and making melody in your
heart to the Lord.*

Ephesians 5:18 KJV

(I remember when Dom Baron was teaching us chant: he finally got us really going in the Introit of the fourth Sunday after Easter and I thought we were going to rock the roof off the church. But that was only once—no, we nearly did it again on the following Ascension Day. The text was perfect for it: *Jubilate Deo omnis terra,* "Sing your joy to God all the earth.") *Jubilate:* it is a joy one *cannot contain.* Where is that in our liturgy today? This is the true liturigical shout of triumph, the triumph we know when divine and angelic beauty possess our whole being, in the joy of the risen Christ!

Thomas Merton

There is no place in the service of worship where vanity and bad taste can so intrude as in the singing. There is, first, the improvised second part which one hears almost everywhere. It attempts to give the necessary background, the missing fullness to the soaring unison tone, and thus kills both the words and the tone. There is the bass or the alto who must call everybody's attention to his astonishing range and therefore sings every hymn an octave lower. There is the solo voice that goes swaggering, swelling, blaring, and tremulant from a full chest and drowns out everything else to the glory of its own fine organ. There are the less dangerous foes of congregational singing, the "unmusical," who cannot sing, of whom there are far fewer than we are led to believe. . . . The more we sing, the more joy will we derive from it, but, above all, the more devotion and discipline and joy we put into our singing, the richer will be the blessing that will come to the whole life of the fellowship from singing together.

Dietrich Bonhoeffer

In truth, there is nothing like music to fill the moment with substance, whether it attune the quiet mind to reverence and worship, or whether it make the mobile senses dance in exultation.

Johann Wolfgang von Goethe

As from the Pow'r of Sacred Lays
   The Spheres began to move,
And sang the great Creator's Praise
   To all the bless'd above;
So, when the last and dreadful Hour
This crumbling Pageant shall devour,
The TRUMPET shall be heard on high,
The dead shall live, and the living die,
And MUSICK shall untune the Sky.

John Dryden

Praise the Lord.

Praise God in his sanctuary;
   praise him in his mighty heavens.
Praise him for his acts of power;
   praise him for his surpassing greatness.
Praise him with the sounding of the trumpet,
   praise him with the harp and lyre,
praise him with tambourine and dancing,
   praise him with the strings and flute,
praise him with the clash of cymbals,
   praise him with resounding cymbals.

Let everything that has breath praise the Lord.

Praise the Lord.

Psalm 150 NIV

In Praise
of God
the Redeemer

The Kingdom Within

In Praise of Good News

Wait, you say.
Is the world around us so really great?
From the moment of all beginnings
till now, is it?
How depraved our music has become.
How discordant the horns we toot.
How murky the colors we mix.
How inclined we are toward
worship of technology
rather than molecules and mysteries.
How self-centered our observations turn out.
In other words, the world around us,
the society of our own kind,
give evidence of our terminal sickness.
We are alienated, we are lost.

Wait, I say.
Do not continue without this good news:
We are not the final word. God is.
We need not be lost. He finds us no matter where.
What we have ruined, He can restore.
What we have profaned, He purifies.
The Love we kill, He makes alive.
And He chooses to do it in Person.

Joyce Blackburn

At the beginning God expressed himself. That personal expression, that word, was with God and was God, and he existed with God from the beginning. All creation took place through him, and none took place without him. In him appeared life and this life was the light of mankind. The light still shines in the darkness, and the darkness has never put it out.

A man called John was sent by God as a witness to the light, so that any man who heard his testimony might believe in the light. This man was not himself the light: he was sent simply as a personal witness to that light.

That was the true light which shines on every man as he comes into the world. He came into the world—the world he had created—and the world failed to recognise him. He came into his own creation, and his own people would not accept him. Yet wherever men did accept him he gave them the power to become sons of God. These were the men who truly believed in him, and their birth depended not on the course of nature nor on any impulse or plan of man, but on God.

So the word of God became a human being and lived among us. We saw his splendour (the splendour as of a father's only son), full of grace and truth. . . . Indeed, every one of us has shared in his riches—there is a grace in our lives because of his grace. For while the Law was given by Moses, love and truth came through Jesus Christ. It is true that no one has ever seen God at any time. Yet the divine and only Son, who lives in the closest intimacy with the Father, has made him known.

John 1:1–18
J. B. Phillips

JESOUS AHATONHIA
(Jesus is Born)

'Twas in the moon of winter-time when all the
    birds had fled
That mighty Gitchi Manitou sent angel choirs
    instead.
      Before their light the stars grew dim,
      And wand'ring hunters heard the hymn:

        "Jesus, your King, is born;
        Jesus is born;
        In Excelsis Gloria!"

Within a lodge of broken bark the tender Babe
    was found,
A ragged robe of rabbit skin enwrapped His
    beauty 'round.
      And as the hunter braves drew nigh,
      The angel song rang loud and high:

        "Jesus, your King, is born;
        Jesus is born;
        In Excelsis Gloria!"

The earliest moon of winter-time is not so round
and fair
As was the ring of glory on the helpless Infant
there.
While chiefs from far before Him knelt
With gifts of fox and beaver pelt.

"Jesus, your King, is born;
Jesus is born;
In Excelsis Gloria!"

O, children of the forest free! O, sons of Manitou!
The Holy Child of earth and heav'n is born today
for you.
Come, kneel before the radiant Boy
Who brings you beauty, peace and joy.

"Jesus, your King, is born;
Jesus is born;
In Excelsis Gloria!"

Huron Christmas Carol by Father Jean De Brébeuf, S. J.
English interpretation by J. E. Middleton

Oh, hearken, for this is wonder!
Light looked down and beheld Darkness;
"Thither will I go," said Light.
Peace looked down and beheld war.
"Thither will I go," said Peace.
Love looked down and beheld Hatred.
"Thither will I go," said Love.
So came Light, and shone.
So came Peace, and gave rest.
So came Love, and brought life.
And the Word was made Flesh, and dwelt among
    us.

Laurence Housman

Matthew 1:1. The book of the genealogy of
   Jesus Christ, the son of David, the Son
   of Abraham. . . .

Luke 2:7. And she gave birth to her first-born
   son
and wrapped him in swaddling cloths,
and laid him in a manger,
because there was no place for them in the inn.

It is not true that you went into eclipse after
   creating
the universe and the world of man
and let your creation go its own capricious way.
You did once thrust yourself omnipotently
into the human scene and placed your eternal
   "I Am"
into the seed of a woman with a genealogy.
You made her cry with the pain of your birthing
and the joy "that a child is born into the world."
You curtailed and caged your omnipresence
to a speck of space in your universe,
abridged your Eternal Self to the time space
of one human life cut down in the prime
   of young manhood.
You let yourself be born nude and native
into the nullity and cruelty and rottenness
of life in this world.

Edna Hong

And the angel said unto them, Fear not: for, behold, I bring you good tidings of great joy, which shall be to all people. For unto you is born this day in the city of David a Saviour, which is Christ the Lord.

Luke 2:10–11 KJV

Too often we think of religion as merely a matter of being good or of keeping difficult rules. But Christianity is never that—it is Good News. It is not good news to be told that you are a sinner. You probably know that already. But it *is* Good News to be told that you can stand up and walk forward as a son or daughter of God because there is a living dependable power, the power of Christ, readily available for you. God has not changed through the centuries . . . the Good News comes to us. God offers us through Christ the reconciliation we could never make, the forgiveness we could never earn—that sense of being at one with God which all our strivings can never produce. And, what is more, if we are prepared to open our hearts and minds to the living Spirit of Christ, he will transform us from within.

This is no conjuring trick, but it is a miracle. For the very thing which all the clever people in the world say—"You can't change human nature"—is proved to be false by the thousands and thousands of people who have proved the living power of Christ.

J. B. Phillips

Strong is the lion—like a coal
His eyeball, like a bastion's mole
   His chest against the foes;
Strong, the gier-eagle on his sail,
Strong against tide, the enormous whale
   Emerges as he goes.

But stronger still, in earth and air
And in the sea, the man of prayer,
   And far beneath the tide;
And in the seat to faith assigned,
Where ask is have, where seek is find,
   Where knock is open wide.

Glorious the sun in mid career;
Glorious the assembled fires appear;
   Glorious the comet's train;
Glorious the trumpet and alarm;
Glorious the almighty stretched-out arm;
   Glorious the enraptured main;

Glorious the northern lights a-stream;
Glorious the song, when God's the theme;
   Glorious the thunder's roar;
Glorious hosanna from the den,
Glorious the catholic amen;
   Glorious the martyr's gore.

Glorious—more glorious, is the crown
Of him that brought salvation down,
   By meekness, called thy Son;
Thou that stupendous truth believed,
And now the matchless deed's achieved,
   DETERMINED, DARED, and DONE.

Christopher Smart

Any word that comes from God is news!

But our ideas of news, the newspapers' idea of news, might lead us to believe that any word *except* what came from God was news. As if what was said by God had to be so fixed, so determined, so rigid in its set form that it could never be anything new, never unpredictable, never astonishing, never frightening. If there is no risk in revelation, if there is no fear in it, if there is no challenge in it, if it is not a word which creates whole new worlds, and new beings, if it does not call into existence a new creature, our new self, then religion is dead and God is dead. Those for whom the Gospel is old, and old *only,* have killed it for the rest of men. The life of the Gospel is its newness. . . . What makes the Gospel news? The faith, which is created in us by God and with which we hear it as news. This acceptance of faith, this new birth in the Spirit, opens up a new dimension in which time and eternity meet, in which all things are made new: eternity, time, our own self, the world around us.

Thomas Merton

Some say that ever 'gainst that season comes
Wherein our Savior's birth is celebrated,
The bird of dawning singeth all night long:
And then, they say, no spirit dare stir abroad;
The nights are wholesome; then no planets
    strike,
No fairy takes, nor witch hath power to charm,
So hallow'd and so gracious is the time.

William Shakespeare

The "good news" has always been, and will always be, that God is discoverable. He is not asking us to follow Him with no notion of what He is really like. He went to the greatest lengths to show Himself as He is. He seemed determined to leave no loopholes. God Himself has already done everything in His power to make Himself known to us.

This is the "good news."

In Praise of God the Redeemer

Bared to
total desolation, shame,
ingratitude, arrogance,
desire, brutality,
greed, rebellion,
cynicism, deceit—
total sin—
is God.
Thorn-circled,
spiked, marred,
hung on the sign of death
to prove Total Love:
love given away
without discrimination, competition,
price or profit,
love forgiving,
remaking us whole again,
fit for His kingdom,
His friendship,
His everlasting life.

Joyce Blackburn

He grew up before him like a tender shoot,
    and like a root out of dry ground.
He had no beauty or majesty to attract us to
        him,
    nothing in his appearance that we should
        desire him.
He was despised and rejected by men,
    a man of sorrows, and familiar with
        suffering.
Like one from whom men hide their faces
    he was despised, and we esteemed him not.

Surely he took up our infirmities
    and carried our sorrows,
yet we considered him stricken by God,
    smitten by him, and afflicted.
But he was pierced for our transgressions,
    he was crushed for our iniquities;
the punishment that brought us peace was
        upon him,
    and by his wounds we are healed.
We all, like sheep, have gone astray,
    each of us has turned to his own way;
and the LORD has laid on him
    the iniquity of us all.

Isaiah 53:2–6 NIV

We don't praise God by flattery—by merely forming words that label Him as great, all-knowing, a God of power, of wisdom, of grace—of glory. He is all these things. And often, in order to salve our consciences, we speak the words and "feel better" because we've "praised" God. Speaking complimentary words *can* stir our minds to remembering that indeed each word is true of God's character, but we truly praise Him *only* by being His friends. "Henceforth, I call you not servants . . . I have called you friends."

Now, once you honestly reach this conclusion that Christ was God—God revealed as fully as is possible, in a human being—you certainly don't know all the answers, but you have a remarkable amount of light to live by. For one thing, it revolutionises your conception of the character of God. You don't see him any longer as a remote and terrifying being insulated from human life. You see him as God who *so loved Man* that *he became Man*. It was not a put-up job. He did it properly, without supernatural advantages, and he lived and died in the sweat and pain of human life, This is not one of those pagan legends about one of the gods disguised as a human being: *this is the real thing.* And once you see what God really was and did and suffered, you begin to see what kind of a person he is, and you have a powerful clue to his long and patient purpose.

J. B. Phillips

We can praise God with clasped hands,
with open hands, with quiet hands.
We cannot praise Him with clenched fists.

Eugenia Price

Christ came on earth, not to wear the awful
cold beauty of a holy statue, but to be numbered
among the wicked, to die as one of them,
condemned by the pure, He who was beyond
purity and impurity. If Christ is not really my
brother with all my sorrows, with all my burdens
on His shoulder and all my poverty and sadness
in His heart, then there has been no redemption.
Then what happened on the Cross was only
magic, and the miracles were magic without
purpose.

Thomas Merton

O Thou best gift from heaven,
Thou who Thyself hast given,
For Thou hast died—

This hast Thou done for me—
What have I done for Thee,
Thou crucified?

I long to serve Thee more,
Reveal an open door
Saviour, to me.

Then counting all but loss,
I'll glory in Thy cross,
And follow Thee.

Who are you, Jesus—
an Author, tasting the misery of the common
    man
for the sake of experiences that will go into a
    book
he plans to write about suffering?

Sage and Founder of a School of Suffering,
walking about in sandals, reciting its gospel
among the poor and lowly and suffering of the
    world?

Bearded Social Activist agonizing
over the problem of suffering
and railing on the streetcorners against the
    injustices
and wickedness that cause suffering?

Preacher denouncing this accursed present
    generation
and ascribing all suffering to its sinfulness?

Government Fact Finder making a study
of human needs in a given area
with a view to drafting a new program to be called
    ACTION?

Knight of Resignation and Despair
going around and making the most
of a rotten situation?

You are none of these!
You are simply and solely God's I Am
incarnate in the flesh.
When you accepted human form,
you accepted evil and suffering
as a fact of life in this world.
The alchemy of No, of nonacceptance,
produces hatred, hostility, harshness, bitterness,
    malice.
The alchemy of your Yes to existential suffering
produced a compassion such as the world has
    never seen,
a life of living, loving, and giving
such as the world has never known.
You wasted no time agonizing over
the great wound of pain and suffering in creation
or in asking who dealt this wound.
You simply accepted it as the mystery of
    existence
and then devoted your life to healing it.
The crowd read in your eyes God's love for
them in their miserable condition
and flocked to you. The crowd laid bare
its painful, suffering wound,
and you touched the wound with your hand,
your most personal human hand—
and healed it.

No gospel of suffering in the Gospels, then—
just you—God's Yes to a suffering world.
No illumination of pain and suffering in the
    Gospels—
just you, God's I Am Love
radiantly and utterly illuminated.

Edna Hong

I bind unto myself today
The power of God to hold and lead,
His eye to watch, His might to stay,
His ear to hearken to my need,
The wisdom of my God to teach,
His hand to guide, His shield to ward;
The word of God to give me speech,
His heavenly host to be my guard.

I bind unto myself the name,
The strong name of the Trinity;
By invocation of the same
The Three in One and One in Three,
Of whom all nature hath creation;
Eternal Father, Spirit, Word;
Praise to the Lord of my salvation,
Salvation is of CHRIST the LORD.

Ascribed to St. Patrick

In the crucifixion of Jesus,
the controversy between God and man
was brought to a head
so it is clear, even to us, that we are sinners
in not honoring God as God,
and in permitting life to revolve around ourselves
instead of Him.
On the other hand, the cross was
God's supreme gesture of reconciliation,
by which He shows, through Christ,
that He is completely free from vindictiveness
and that He desires only reconciliation.
Through the cross
God wiped out every charge
which was based on the requirements of the law,
because Christ died for our sins.
Having done all this,
He invites us to recognize that we are sinners
in rebellion against Him . . .
and to turn against our own sin
and accept His complete pardon.
He will hold our sins against us no longer.
We are actually redeemed from the dominion of
    sin
through the cross.
The price of our redemption or ransom
is the blood of Christ.
Sin loses its power
to blind us to the sinfulness of our rebellion
against God so that we may come repentant,
seeking His pardon.
Sin also loses its power to condemn us,
for God now holds nothing against us.
This is what the cross really means.

Wesley Nelson

When I survey the wondrous cross
On which the Prince of Glory died,
My richest gain I count but loss,
And pour contempt on all my pride.

Forbid it, Lord, that I should boast,
Save in the death of Christ, my God;
All the vain things that charm me most,
I sacrifice them to his blood.

See, from his head, his hands, his feet,
Sorrow and love flow mingled down;
Did e'er such love and sorrow meet,
Or thorns compose so rich a crown?

Were the whole realm of nature mine,
That were an offering far too small;
Love so amazing, so divine,
Demands my soul, my life, my all. Amen.

Isaac Watts

The death of Jesus Christ is the performance in history of the very Mind of God. There is no room for looking on Jesus Christ as a martyr; His death was not something that happened to Him which might have been prevented: His death was the very reason why He came. . . . The greatest note of triumph that ever sounded in the ears of a startled universe was that sounded on the Cross of Christ—*"It is finished."* That is the last word in the Redemption of man.

Oswald Chambers

You cannot martyr God. God could not have his life taken from him. Hold in mind all the time who it was who hung and suffered there, and you will not think of it as martyrdom.

If he was man, it was murder; if he was God, it was an offering.

If he was man, it was martyrdom; if he was God, it was sacrifice.

If he was man, they took his life from him; if he was God, he laid it down of himself.

If he was man, we are called to admiration; if he was God, we are called to adoration.

If he was man, we must stand up and take our hats off; if he was God, we must fall down and give him our hearts.

If you come to Calvary with some admiration of his life and some pity at his death, and see in him nothing but another good man beaten by the wickedness of the world, you have not really come to Calvary at all. No mere man could save you. The teaching of the Church Universal is this: the immortal God has died for you.

W. E. Sangster

*He saved others; himself he cannot save. If he
be the King of Israel, let him now come down
from the cross, and we will believe him.*

Matthew 27:42

Himself he cannot save. . . ." Himself He *could*
not afford to save! If He had saved Himself, He
could not have saved us. If His prayer that the cup
might pass from Him had been answered in the
affirmative, our prayers could never be answered
at all!

All His earthly life, Jesus had walked long,
weary miles, pouring His humanity out to those
who needed a shepherd. Healing, teaching,
admonishing, showing His love. Now, some of
the same lost sheep to whom He had been giving
of His strength and love were there beneath the
Cross jeering at Him! In His deep love and
concern for their eternal lives, "Jesus (had) stood
and cried, saying, If any man thirst, let him come
unto me, and drink." Now, those to whom He
cried, jeered at Him, "Let him come down from
the cross, and (then) we will believe him."

Does this sound familiar to you? "If God will
just do this thing which I want so much, *then* I'll
believe Him."

He did not die to give us what *we* want. He
died to give us eternal life. An exchange of lives.
His for ours. An exchange of cries . . . His cry
for ours! We cry for Him to do this and that
and *then* we will begin to "believe." We will
"condescend" to believe in the Son of God on
our terms. This blessed Son of God, now alive
forever, knew that *sin* prompts a cry like ours.
And so when He died, He cried in response to
our cry: "It is finished!" It *is* finished.

Eugenia Price

Jesus is God stepping out of the frame of the universe and coming to me intimately and personally. He is God pressing home upon my heart the pressures of his heart. He is God breaking through . . . breaking through to my understanding and my heart. He is love seeking its own . . . its own: ME. Jesus is God become understandable and loveable. He is the Personal Approach from the unseen.

E. Stanley Jones

The God who created the world
*   and everything in it, and*
who is Lord of heaven and earth,
*   does not live in shrines*
made by men. . . . He is not far
*   from each one of us, for in him*
we live and move, in him we exist.

Acts 17:24, 28 NEB

They borrowed a bed to lay His head
   When Christ the Lord came down;
They borrowed the ass in the mountain pass
   For Him to ride to town;
But the Crown that He wore and the Cross that
     He bore
   Were His own—
   The Cross was His own.

He borrowed the bread when the crowd He fed
   On the grassy mountain side;
He borrowed the dish of broken fish
   With which He satisfied;
But the Crown that He wore and the Cross that
     He bore
   Were His own—
   The Cross was His own.

He borrowed the ship in which to sit
   To teach the multitude;
He borrowed a nest in which to rest,
   He had never a home so crude;
But the Crown that He wore and the Cross that
     He bore
   Were His own—
   The Cross was His own.

He borrowed a room on His way to the tomb,
   The Passover Lamb to eat;
They borrowed a cave for Him a grave;
   They borrowed a winding sheet;
But the Crown that He wore and the Cross that
     He bore
   Were His own—
   The Cross was His own.

Now Christ is the visible expression of the invisible God. He existed before creation began, for it was through him that everything was made, whether spiritual or material, seen or unseen. Through him, and for him, also, were created power and dominion, ownership and authority. In fact, every single thing was created through, and for, him. He is both the first principle and the upholding principle of the whole scheme of creation. And now he is the head of the body which is the Church. Life from nothing began through him, and life from the dead began through him, and he is, therefore, justly called the Lord of all. It was in him that the full nature of God chose to live, and through him God planned to reconcile in his own person, as it were, everything on earth and everything in Heaven by virtue of the sacrifice of the cross.

Colossians 1:15–20
J. B. Phillips

*For the love of Christ leaves us no choice,
    when once we have reached the conclusion
that one man died for all and therefore
    all mankind has died. His purpose in
dying for all was that men, while still in life,
    should cease to live for themselves,
and should live for him who for their sake
    died and was raised to life.*

2 Corinthians 5:14–15 NEB

Creator, Eternal One,
Sun of my Soul,
Guardian of the Way,
Lord, Jehovah, King,
No word can capture you,
but still I try.

Marks on paper,
empty,
mock me.
What do I know,
in my self-sufficiency,
of you?

Then, bewildered,
I stray in circles,
feel earth quake beneath my feet,
shake in witless terror
of the unknown,
and cry at last,
"I am lost! Save me."

Helpless,
stripped of my pride,
naked in my need,
arrogance dissolved in fear,
I surrender,
And wait for you to capture me.

And in the joy of being found
I find the word.
I whisper,
"Savior."

Olive Anderson

If I could praise God for only one event in human history, it would be the moment He decided that there simply was no other way for Him to make it clear to us what His nature really is like except to become one of us. Redemption springs from the very nature of God. Perhaps He did not even have to decide, as we think of deciding, that there would be no other way for us to catch on except that He enter human history in the Person of Jesus Christ. Whether God made that decision is not important. What matters is that He *did* come. And that event, above all others, opens human understanding. Once we understand, even a little, we are free to act. I became a believer at the moment of my own acceptance of the *fact* that God is knowable in Jesus. New knowledge of Him may come to us throughout all eternity. Certainly it is unending on this earth. *But we can know.* We *can* know of his intentions toward the whole human race. We *can* know the quality of His love. Because the young Man hung there on His cross with His arms stretched out to the whole world, we can know all we need to know of the heart of God.

If, no matter how long we've been believers, we are still amazed, still set spinning that the Eternal Creator God would bother to such an extent—we are, in that moment of spinning, of helpless amazement, praising Him.

Eugenia Price

No one ever needs to fear God's recoil from anything. Or anyone.

The thief on the cross who turned to Jesus found this to be true. The Lord knew this man's heart and knew why his criminal record was what it was. He was not shocked that the man dared to ask from a criminal's cross to be remembered when Christ came into His Kingdom. Jesus was nailed to the same kind of cross. He could not reach His hand to the fellow; it was nailed down. But He was still Love. And His love reached out and assured the thief that with no further delay or ceremony, he would be with Him that very day in Paradise.

He moved toward the penitent thief that dark afternoon with all the love of His breaking heart. But to those who know Him as He is, this is just what one would expect Him to do. After all, God is Love. And love is always in motion toward the loved one. To be shocked is to recoil.

Love never recoils. It reaches out to heal.

Eugenia Price

O Cross, more splendid than all the stars,
Glorious to the world,
Greatly to be loved by men,
More holy than all things that are,
Thou who alone wast worthy to weigh the gold of
    the world's ransom,
Sweet tree, beloved nails,
Bearing the Love-Burden,
Save us who have come together here, this day,
In choirs for Thy Praise!
Alleluia, alleluia, alleluia!

Thomas Merton

In Praise of Vital Truth

Before the Sabbath, I stood guard.
My orders were strict:
This corpse is cold, rigid
as a slaughtered lamb,
still, take no chance.
Make the new tomb fast.
Fix the stone in place.
Seal it against weather,
thieves and fans.
Set the watch.
This liar is dead.

After the Sabbath, an angel replaced me.
I had not believed in angels, either,
but who else has lightning
burning from the brow?
Who else could roll the stone aside
and perch upon it?
For myself, I can see
the tomb is empty,
the linen wraps cast off.
The angel is right. God is not dead.
He is alive!
And that is the truth.
Yes, I witness to the truth.
He is risen, just as He said.

Joyce Blackburn

No tabloid will ever print the startling news that the mummified body of Jesus of Nazareth has been discovered in old Jerusalem.

Christians have no carefully embalmed body enclosed in a glass case to worship.

Thank God, we have an empty tomb.

The glorious fact that the empty tomb proclaims to us is that life for us does not stop when death comes.

Death is not a wall, but a door.

And eternal life which may be ours now, by faith in Christ, is not interrupted when the soul leaves the body, for we live on . . . and on.

There is no death to those who have entered into fellowship with Him who emerged from the tomb.

Because the Resurrection is true, it is the most significant thing in our world today.

Peter Marshall

Either Jesus never was or He still is. . . . If the story . . . had ended on Golgotha, it would indeed be of a Man Who Died, but as two thousand years later the Man's promise that *where two or three are gathered together in my name, there am I in the midst of them,* manifestly still holds, it is actually the story of a Man Who Lives.

Malcolm Muggeridge

So they went, and made the sepulchre sure, sealing the stone, and setting a watch.
Matthew 27:66

They carefully selected a huge boulder. Rolled it against the open tomb, sealed it, and placed a hand-picked guard of soldiers to watch the grave of Jesus. They "made the sepulchre sure." They made sure, to their own satisfaction, that the body of Jesus would never be seen again. Jesus had said He would rise again and the chief priests and Pharisees urged Pilate to take all possible precautions to see that His disciples didn't steal His body and then spread the story that He had risen. So, they "made the sepulchre sure." Completely sure, they thought.

But, glory to God in the very highest, the *only* thing that was really sure was that Jesus was going to get up under the power of God and walk out of that sealed tomb! He didn't roll the stone away in order to get out. He didn't need to. The stone was not even rolled away until "the end of the sabbath, as it began to dawn toward the first day of the week." The guards were still there, the stone was still in place, but Jesus was gone. The stone was merely rolled back so that when His disciples came they could see *inside* and know that He had told them the truth.

They "made the sepulchre sure" against themselves only. Jesus Christ Himself could not have been "sealed in" by a mere stone, because He Himself *is* Eternal Life.

Eugenia Price

O Christ, Thy empty tomb makes all our fears lies and all our hopes truths. Thy empty tomb is the birthplace of eternal certainty. I thank Thee.

Jesus didn't use the word immortality. . . . He spoke of "eternal life," and that meant life not merely in eternal duration, but in a quality so rich, so inexhaustible, so abundant now that it simply could not be confined to this life. Eternal life is a quality of life as different from the ordinary life as the ordinary life is different from the animal. That quality of life bursts the bonds of death as a seed rends a rock. . . .

No wonder the early Christians shut up within dark underground prisons wrote on the walls . . . "Vita, Vita, Vita"—"Life, Life, Life." Prison walls could not stifle or quench this life, nor can death extinguish it. By its very nature it is bound to go beyond the borders of this life. Can the shell confine the growing seed? Can death stop the Christian? Stop him? It only frees him—forever.

E. Stanley Jones

For you know that it was not with perishable things such as silver or gold that you were redeemed from the empty way of life handed down to you from your forefathers, but with the precious blood of Christ, a lamb without blemish or defect. He was chosen before the creation of the world, but was revealed in these last times for your sake. Through him you believe in God, who raised him from the dead and glorified him, and so your faith and hope are in God.

1 Peter 1:18–21 NIV

Hurrah. Hurrah.
Hurray.
Old things are made new.
The corruptible becomes incorruptible.
The mortal becomes immortal.
Redemption is very near.
It is here.
It is a new day.
The former things have passed away.
The Son of God
draws all life to himself.
Renewal is previewed in the truth that
the precious pod shall burst
and the seed shall rot and die
and be transformed
into a new leaf and a new stem
and a new bloom.
Hurrah. New life has come.
It is true for the flower
yearly,
for the dead
once,
and for the living
daily.
Hurray for life.

Herbert Brokering

If anyone is in Christ,
he is a new creation.

2 Corinthians 5:17 NIV

Christianity is not that complex system of oppressive rules which the unbeliever describes; it is peace, joy, love, and a life which is continually renewed, like the mysterious pulse of nature at the beginning of Spring. We must assert this truth as confidently as the Apostles did, and you . . . must be convinced of it, for it is your greatest treasure, which alone can give meaning and serenity to your daily life.

The source of this joy is in the Risen Christ, who has set man free from the slavery of sin and invites him to become a new creature with Him, and to look forward to an eternity of joy.

Pope John XXIII

Spring bursts today,
For Christ is risen and all the earth's at play.

Flash forth, thou sun,
The rain is over and gone, its work is done.

Winter is past,
Sweet spring is come at last, is come at last.

Bud, fig and vine,
Bud, olive, fat with fruit and oil, and wine.

Break forth this morn
In roses, thou but yesterday a thorn.

Uplift thy head,
O pure white lily through the winter dead.

Beside your dams
Leap and rejoice, you merry-making lambs.

All herds and flocks
Rejoice, all beasts of thickets and of rocks.

Sing, creatures, sing,
Angels and men and birds, and everything. . . .

Christina G. Rossetti

Praise be to the God and Father of Our Lord Jesus Christ! In his great mercy he has given us new birth into a living hope through the resurrection of Jesus Christ from the dead, and into an inheritance that can never perish, spoil or fade—kept in heaven for you, who through faith are shielded by God's power until the coming of the salvation that is ready to be revealed in the last time. In this you greatly rejoice, though now for a little while you may have had to suffer grief in all kinds of trials. These have come so that your faith—of greater worth than gold, which perishes even though refined by fire—may be proved genuine and may result in praise, glory and honor when Jesus Christ is revealed. Though you have not seen him, you love him; and even though you do not see him now, you believe in him and are filled with an inexpressible and glorious joy, for you are receiving the goal of your faith, the salvation of your souls.

1 Peter 1:3–9 NIV

In my risen Lord I am born into "a living hope," a hope not only vital, but vitalizing, sending its mystic, vivifying influences through every highway and by-way of my soul.

In my risen Lord mine is *"an inheritance incorruptible."* It is not exposed to the gnawing tooth of time. Moth and rust cannot impair the treasure. It will not grow less as I grow old. Its glories are as invulnerable as my Lord.

In my risen Lord mine is "an inheritance *undefiled*." There is no alloy in the fine gold. The King will give me of His best.

And mine is "an inheritance that *fadeth not away*." It shall not be as the garlands offered by men—green today and tomorrow sere and yellow. "Its leaf also shall not whither." It shall always retain its freshness, and shall offer me a continually fresh delight. And these are all mine in Him!

"Thou, O Christ, art all I want."

John Henry Jowett

Jesus said, "He that heareth my word, and believeth on him that sent me, hath everlasting life." Notice the force of the present tense, "*hath* everlasting life." The moment a man's central confidence is shifted from his own efforts to the God who made him, he is linked to the timeless life of God himself, that is, eternal life. To put it bluntly, heaven is not, as we might deduce from some hymns, a "reward for being a good boy." It is continuance and expansion of a quality of life already imparted to the man who believes in Christ and follows his way.

J. B. Phillips

EASTER

Most glorious Lord of lyfe, that, on this day,
  Didst make thy triumph over death and sin;
And, having harrowed hell, didst bring away
  Captivity, thence captive, us to win:
  This joyous day, deare Lord, with joy begin;
And grant that we, for whom thou diddest dye,
  Being with thy deare blood clene washt from
    sin,
May live for ever in felicity.
And that thy love we weighing worthily,
  May likewise love thee for the same againe;
And for thy sake, that all lyke deare didst buy,
  With love may one another entertayne!
    So let us love, deare Love, lyke as we ought,
    —Love is the lesson which the Lord us
     taught.

Edmund Spenser

Jesus Christ is risen today,
    Alleluia!
Our triumphant holy day,
    Alleluia!
Who did once, upon the cross,
    Alleluia!
Suffer to redeem our loss.
    Alleluia!

Hymns of praise then let us sing,
    Alleluia!
Unto Christ, our heavenly King,
    Alleluia!
Who endured the cross and grave,
    Alleluia!
Sinners to redeem and save.
    Alleluia!

Sing we to our God above,
    Alleluia!
Praise eternal as his love;
    Alleluia!
Praise him, all ye heavenly host,
    Alleluia!
Father, Son, and Holy Ghost.
    Alleluia!

Latin, 14th Century

Whoever lives and believes in me will never die.

John 11:26 NIV

Eternal life is *eternal* life.

It is the very life of God Himself. "I am the resurrection *and the life* ... I am the way, the truth *and the life."* Jesus did not say He would show us a better *way* of life. He is *not* a "way-shower" as the modern cult would have us believe.

He, Himself, *is* the way.

He, Himself, *is* the life.

That's why we can know that when Jesus walks up to a man or woman dead in sin, life inevitably results. *If* that person *believes* in Jesus as eternal life itself. Where He is, death cannot remain. Things and people spring to life around Jesus. It's inevitable.

Any man or woman who *believes* in Jesus Christ simply *cannot* die. "Whosoever believeth in him shall not perish, but have everlasting life." God's life. And He is eternal. He goes on. So do we, if we have received His life into ours. We can no more stop than God can stop! Eternal life *is* everlasting life. It lasts *forever.*

Eugenia Price

Since, then, you have been raised with Christ,
set your hearts on things above,
where Christ is seated at the right hand of God.
Set your minds on things above,
not on earthly things. For you died,
and your life is now hidden with Christ in God.
When Christ, who is your life, appears,
then you also will appear with him in glory.

Colossians 3:1–4

Universe
and every universe beyond,
spin and blaze,
whirl and dance,
leap and laugh
as never before.
It's happened.
It's new.
It's here.
The liberation.
The victory.
The new creation.
Christ has smashed death.
He has liberated the world.
He has freed the universe.
You and I and everything
are free again,
new again,
alive again.

Let's have a festival
and follow him across the skies,
through the flames of heaven
and back down every alley in our town.
There, let's have him come
to liberate our city,
clean up the mess
and start all over again.
You conquered.
Keep on fighting through us.

You arose.
Keep rising in us.
You celebrated.
Keep on celebrating with us.
You happen.
You are new.
You are here.

Norman C. Habel

In Praise of Power

Since Your coming
there has been no shortage
of power and presence
available to the family of God.
You come now, as then,
the rush of wind
demolishing our shallow pretense,
the tongues of flame
burning our false piety to ash,
purifying the very climate
in which we grow.
Our sin-inflicted wounds
You heal,
our ruptured, bereaved minds
You comfort,
hidden and ultimate truth
You teach.
Oh, Breath of God,
guide us—whether silent or shouting—
to give witness to the force of love.
We praise You, yes,
and the Father,
and the Son,
Blessed Trinity!

Joyce Blackburn

According to the Book of Acts, the Christian experience of the Holy Spirit is one of *realized presence.* Being "filled with the Spirit" (Acts 2:4) means a conspicuous relation with God; it means an understood share in his will. It includes an awareness of relationship and being engaged by God.

The biblical doctrine of the Holy Spirit is one of the richest teachings found in Scripture. This doctrine is not a mere leftover from the Jewish background of the first Christians. The biblical doctrine of the Holy Spirit is an emphatic statement about how God shares himself with us inwardly. It tells us about how God penetrates our lives by his presence, participating with us in the details and drama of living. The doctrine about the Holy Spirit contains deep truths about an essential matter: how God interacts with our human spirit, sharing his mind, his character, his guidance, his love, his helping hand. One noted theologian once traced all the biblical references to the Holy Spirit and summed them up within two expressions: God-at-hand, *intimacy,* and God-at-work, *potency.*

James E. Massey

In the words of Scripture, "Things beyond our seeing, things beyond our hearing, things beyond our imagining, all prepared by God for those who love him," these it is that God has revealed to us through the Spirit.

For the Spirit explores everything, even the depths of God's own nature.

1 Corinthians 2:9–11 NEB

Jesus told His disciples, *"It is to your advantage* that I go away, for if I do not go away, the Counselor will not come to you; but if I go, I will send him to you"* (John 16:7).

We can understand that now. How thankful we should be that He is here in the Spirit rather than as a mere human being. He is no longer limited by humanity. People can have Him in Nazareth, Jerusalem, Chicago, Boston, and we can have Him just as truly wherever we are.

He is *here now.* More than nineteen hundred years later, He is with us and others all around the world. Now we can know that the Holy Spirit is not a substitute for an absent Lord but the agent and mediator of His living Presence.

Peter saw what many Christians today do not realize—that this gift of the Holy Spirit is a norm in the God experience for every Christian. That means it was not for the apostles only, nor for the people in the upper room only, nor for the people of that day only, but for all of us from that day to this who love the Lord Jesus Christ and become His fully committed followers.

The outward evidences and manifestations on the day of Pentecost were minor compared with the power released in the lives of otherwise insignificant people. The outward evidences were a joy to experience and to remember, but the new consciousness of the *Presence* in their lives and community was so wonderful that they understood now what Jesus meant when He said it was better for Him to leave so the Spirit could come. It took the whole book of Acts and the Letters of the New Testament to tell what had really happened on the day of Pentecost.

Anna B. Mow

Our blest Redeemer, ere He breathed
　　His tender last farewell,
A Guide, a Comforter bequeathed,
　　With us to dwell.

He came in tongues of living flame,
　　To teach, convince, subdue;
All-powerful as the wind He came,
　　As viewless too.

He came sweet influence to impart,
　　A gracious, willing Guest,
While He can find one humble heart
　　Wherein to rest.

And His that gentle voice we hear,
　　Soft as the breath of even,
That checks each fault, that calms each fear,
　　And speaks of heaven.

And every virtue we possess,
　　And every victory won,
And every thought of holiness
　　Are His alone.

Spirit of purity and grace,
　　Our weakness pitying see;
O make our hearts Thy dwelling-place,
　　And worthier Thee.

Harriet Auber

There are three facts about God:
    God *for* us,
    God *with* us,
    God *in* us.
God *for* us, the divine Intention,
    the Father;
God *with* us, the divine Invasion,
    the Son;
God *in* us, the divine Indwelling,
    the Holy Spirit.

The divine Intention becomes the divine Invasion, and the divine Invasion becomes the divine Indwelling. It is not enough to have redemptive Intention and redemptive Invasion. They are both outside of us, therefore inadequate, for our need is within us. There must be Indwelling.

What happened in history in the Incarnation must move straight on inside of us in experience in the Indwelling, must do it or fail. The historical must become the experimental. Otherwise the Christian faith is a counsel of perfection, making impossible demands on human nature. But if the divine Indwelling is a fact, then everything is possible.

E. Stanley Jones

The Holy Spirit will minister to me as a *wind*. He will create an atmosphere in my life which will quicken all sweet and beautiful growth. And this shall be my native air. Gracious seeds, which have never awaked, shall now unfold themselves, and "the desert shall rejoice and blossom as the rose." It was a saying of Huxley, that if our little island were to be invaded by tropical airs, tropical seeds which are now lying dormant in English gardens and fields would troop out of their graves in bewildering wealth and beauty! "Breathe on me, breath of God!"

John Henry Jowett

Spirit of the living God, fall fresh on me;
Spirit of the living God, fall fresh on me.
Break me! Melt me! Mold me! Fill me!
Spirit of the living God, fall fresh on me.

Daniel Iverson

In Praise of Love

To think, the proof of my discipleship
is love—my loving you!
Not out of preference
or reasonableness
or obligation
or conscience
or sympathy,
not my natural love
but God's supernatural variety,
wild, risky,
never playing it safe,
no calculated dividends—
no thank-yous even—
no hedging on forgiveness (70 x 7 = 490),
no insurance against breakage,
no promise of survival (put your life on the line,
He says, lay it down for a friend),
nothing less will do,
nothing less than flat out surrender of my rights
for the good of my soul-mates
in the kingdom of love.

And do not be naïve, He will not stop there.
Once His own love is expressed in me,
He will woo me into more and beyond—
way beyond—including the impossible
neighbor, enemy, bigot, leper, outlaw, snob,
cynic, moron, whoever, "the world"—
there will be no end to it!
Nothing less than giving away
all the love He has.
Nothing less will do:
my abandoned YES
to His infinite heart.

Joyce Blackburn

To love at all is to be vulnerable. Love anything, and your heart will certainly be wrung and possibly be broken. If you want to make sure of keeping it intact, you must give your heart to no one, not even to an animal. Wrap it carefully round with hobbies and little luxuries; avoid all entanglements; lock it up safe in the casket or coffin of your selfishness. But in that casket—safe, dark, motionless, airless—it will change. It will not be broken; it will become unbreakable, impenetrable, irredeemable. The alternative to tragedy, or at least to the risk of tragedy, is damnation. The only place outside Heaven where you can be perfectly safe from all the dangers and perturbations of love is Hell.

C. S. Lewis

He saw our masses and rosaries and prayer meetings and study groups and devotions, and he said yes, yes, yes, you are quite right to think that goodness demands rigor and vigilance and observance, but your new moons and sabbaths and bullocks and altars and vestments and Gospel teams and taboos and Bible studies are trumpery, and they nauseate me because you have elevated *them,* and I alone am the Host. Your incense is foetid, and your annotated Bibles are rubbish paper. Your meetings are a bore and your myopic exegesis is suffocating.

Return, return, and think again what I have asked of you: to follow justice, and love mercy, and do your job of work, and love one another, and give me the worship of your heart—your *heart*—and be merry and thankful and lowly and not pompous and gaunt and sere.

Thomas Howard

Love has many voices. Love sends its greeting in the smile of a friend, the contented sighs of a baby, the felt whisperings of the Spirit.

Often we are slow to recognize how many voices are really love's voice.

"God is love," says John the Evangelist. "He who dwells in love is dwelling in God, and God in him."

Love speaks in many places. It leans against the neighbor's fence or comes sniffing into a kitchen filled with cooking. It walks amid the bustle of the city streets or stands on a crowded bus.

Love has many moods. Sometimes love is bold and happy or else it is anxious and hesitant. Sometimes it is riotous and demanding, or gentle and relaxed, or even sober and practical. Sometimes love just waits.

Love comes in all seasons. It rides the icy winds of winter and laughs with raindrops in the spring. It wanders through the restless heat of summer and catches leaves of autumn as they fall.

Listen to love.

Louis M. Senery

I will not quarrel with you about my opinion;
only see that your heart is right toward God, that
you know and love the Lord Jesus Christ; that
you love your neighbor, and walk as your Master
walked, and I desire no more. I am sick of
opinions; am weary to bear them; my soul
loathes this frothy food. Give me solid and
substantial religion; give me a humble, gentle
lover of God and man; a man full of mercy
and good faith, without partiality and without
hypocrisy; a man laying himself out in the work of
faith, the patience of hope, the labour of love. Let
my soul be with these Christians wheresoever
they are, and whatsoever opinion they are of!

John Wesley

The gifts of love one wants to make change, but the desire to make them remains the only real happiness I know anything about. I am not speaking of joy now, which comes unbidden and is unaccountable, but of love and its accountable accompaniment. And this happiness has nothing to do with being loved. "Being loved" is something that happens to someone else. Loving is what happens to you. Without it and the desire that always goes with it to make gifts of love, life is maimed, mutilated, deprived, depraved. Without it, life is soured at the source. With it, anything can be borne. To live without being loved is sorrowful. Without loving there *is* no real life.

Jessamyn West

Nearly all seek themselves in thy gifts, instead of seeking thee alone by the cross. . . . We want to guide thee, instead of letting ourselves be guided by thee. We give ourselves to thee to become great, but we hold back since we have to let ourselves be made small. We say that we cling to nothing, and we are frightened by the slightest loss. We want to possess thee, but we do not want to lose ourselves so that we can be possessed by thee. This is not loving thee. This is wanting to be loved by thee. O God! The creature does not realize why thou hast made it. Teach it and impress in the depths of its heart that the clay should allow itself unresistantly to take all the shapes that the potter pleases.

Fénelon

It is the work of love to fulfill our lives, not to dispose of them; and so it is that love chooses patience, trust, and goodness. We know that all our days have their dimmings and their nets of failure: we got the contract but lost our honor, we won the fight but hated our enemy, we appeased our passion but injured another, we filled the hours with busyness and lost eternity, we remained engrossed in ourself and in the security of our self-interest though we had to be a snob and betray the trust of another to do it; all was so loud and so busy that the quiet touch and motionless fulfillment of love were absent from the day; we have netted ourselves in a design of doing that binds us in pressure of ways and means, and have made ourselves into a tool for disposing of tomorrow and tomorrow (as Macbeth in despair found he had done), and our dreams at night are dreams of passions, desires, and doings; but when morning returns we may choose to love again, and love returns us to the work of patience, trust, and goodness, bringing warmth and light again into our holy endeavor to abide with God.

For the patience of love is to abide with God. The trust of love is to trust God. And the goodness of love is to respond to God. And it is by this presence of God that the patience, trust, and goodness of love fulfill peace and understanding between us and hallow our communion.

Robert Raynolds

"But as touching brotherly love ye need not that I write unto you: for ye yourselves are taught of God to love one another. . . . but we beseech you, brethren, that ye increase more and more" (1 Thess. 4:9, 10). God Himself has undertaken to teach brotherly love; all that men can add to it is to remember this divine instruction and the admonition to excel in it more and more. When God was merciful, when He revealed Jesus Christ to us as our Brother, when He won our hearts by His love, this was the beginning of our instruction in divine love. When God was merciful to us, we learned to be merciful with our brethren. When we received forgiveness instead of judgment, we, too, were made ready to forgive our brethren. What God did to us, we then owed to others. The more we received, the more we were able to give; and the more meager our brotherly love, the less were we living by God's mercy and love. Thus God Himself taught us to meet one another as God has met us in Christ. "Wherefore receive ye one another, as Christ also received us to the glory of God" (Rom. 15:7).

Dietrich Bonhoeffer

Love bade me welcome; yet my soul drew back,
  Guilty of dust and sin.
But quick-eyed Love, observing me grow slack
  From my first entrance in,
Drew nearer to me, sweetly questioning,
  If I lacked anything.

'A guest,' I answered, 'worthy to be here.'
  Love said, 'You shall be he.'
'I, the unkind, ungrateful? Ah, my dear,
  I cannot look on Thee.'
Love took my hand, and smiling did reply,
  'Who made the eyes but I?'

'Truth, Lord, but I have marred them; let my shame
  Go where it doth deserve.'
'And know you not,' says Love, 'who bore the blame?'
  'My dear, then I will serve.'
'You must sit down,' says Love, 'and taste My meat.'
  So I did sit and eat.

George Herbert

John once asked pertinently, "For he that loveth not his brother whom he hath seen, how can he love God whom he hath not seen?" Of course, if we separate in our minds God and Man, and regard God as wholly Other, the answer is easy. God is unimaginable beauty and goodness; but Man is ignorant, stupid, selfish, and irritating. But if we once digest the truth that God has identified Himself with man in Christ, then we see the force of John's question. We can also realize the force of his bald statement in the same verse, "If a man say, I love God, and hateth his brother, he is a liar." It is unhappily true that quite a number of modern Christians have separated love of God from love of their brothers and sisters. Whenever the Church turns in upon itself and restricts its love to its own members, this fatal split occurs. Whenever the Church turns a blind eye to unfair racial discrimination, or to flagrant snobbery, it is exhibiting exactly the opposite spirit to the spirit of the Incarnation. We may much prefer cut-and-dried schemes of salvation and the comfortable feeling that we are one of the saved, but we may safely infer from the sayings of Jesus that no individual or church finds salvation unless love of God goes hand in hand with love of fellow men.

J. B. Phillips

God has given us His Spirit to guide, comfort, and correct us, and we begin to congratulate ourselves on our spiritual sensitivity. He gave us the Church because we need each other, and we have walled it off and divided it into hundreds of tiny compounds, deciding who is and is not "really" Christian. He gave us the Bible to teach us, and we use it like a bludgeon to beat each other over the head with; and we quote Scripture verses to wound instead of to heal.

Worst of all, we have become "respectable." We talk, in our Christian groups, about being sinners, but with the mental reservation that there are, thank goodness, some sins which we certainly would not be guilty of. No doubt God forgives those who do sin, we mentally add, but though we may meet them in heaven (suitably cleaned up, we trust) we need not mingle with them here.

As long as we cherish the illusion that we have any virtue in ourselves, we are no candidates for God's love. That is for those who need Him, who cannot do without Him and who know it.

Do we want love in our lives? God offers it to us, a measureless ocean of love. Even if no one has ever loved us, He does. There is nothing we can do that will put us beyond it. The only thing that can keep us from it is any illusion that we deserve it. His love is limitless—it is free—and it is unearned. . . .

My comfort and my hope for the future lie in the forgiveness and renewal I find in Christ. It is humiliating but somehow very bracing to face God in prayer, confessing my lack of love, and accepting His cleansing and forgiving and accepting love. I can go on. So can we all, not with any expectation of arriving, some day, at a point of perfection, but with the assurance that our sins are forgiven—first among them our lack of love—and that we are, in daily commitment to Christ, becoming what He has declared us to be.

One last thing. When we have done all we can, spoken and acted the best that we could, there comes a time when one can do no more—except for one thing. We can love. Imperfectly, sometimes stumblingly, we can go on giving ourselves to Christ so that He can give Himself more completely to us. Our love loses its limitedness in His limitless love.

Eileen Guder

God's love tells us that He is friendly and His Word assures us that He is our friend and wants us to be His friends. No man with a trace of humility would first think that he is a friend of God; but the idea did not originate with men. Abraham would never have said, "I am God's friend," but God Himself said that Abraham was His friend. The disciples might well have hesitated to claim friendship with Christ, but Christ said to them, "Ye are my friends." Modesty may demur at so rash a thought, but audacious faith dares to believe the Word and claim friendship with God. We do God more honor by believing what He has said about Himself and having the courage to come boldly to the throne of grace than by hiding in self-conscious humility among the trees of the garden.

Love is also an emotional identification. It considers nothing its own but gives all freely to the object of its affection.

It is a strange and beautiful eccentricity of the free God that He has allowed His heart to be emotionally identified with men. Self-sufficient as He is, He wants our love and will not be satisfied till He gets it. Free as He is, He has let His heart be bound to us forever. "Herein is love, not that we loved God, but that he loved us, and sent his Son to be the propitiation for our sins."

A. W. Tozer

O for a thousand tongues to sing
My great Redeemer's praise,
The glories of my God and King,
The triumphs of His grace.

My gracious Master and my God,
Assist me to proclaim,
To spread through all the earth abroad
The honors of Thy Name.

Jesus! the Name that charms our fears,
That bids our sorrows cease,
'Tis music in the sinner's ears,
'Tis life, and health, and peace.

Glory to God and praise and love,
Be ever, ever given,
By saints below and saints above,
The Church in earth and heaven.

Charles Wesley

I may speak with the tongues of men and of
    angels, but if I have no love,
  I am a noisy gong or a clanging cymbal;
I may prophesy, fathom all mysteries and
    secret lore,
I may have such absolute faith that I can move
    hills from their place,
  but if I have no love,
  I count for nothing;
I may distribute all I possess in charity,
I may give up my body to be burnt,
  but if I have no love,
  I make nothing of it.
Love is very patient, very kind
Love knows no jealousy;
Love makes no parade, gives itself no airs, is
    never rude, never selfish, never irritated,
    never resentful;
Love is never glad when others go wrong,
Love is gladdened by goodness, always slow to
    expose, always eager to believe the best,
    always hopeful, always patient.

Love never disappears.
As for prophesying, it will be superseded.
As for 'tongues,' they will cease;
As for knowledge, it will be superseded.
For we only know bit by bit, and we only
    prophesy bit by bit;
But when the perfect comes, the imperfect will
    be superseded.
When I was a child,
   I talked like a child,
   I thought like a child,
   I argued like a child;
Now that I am a man, I am done with childish
    ways.
At present we only see the baffling reflections
    in a mirror, but then it will be face to face;
At present I am learning bit by bit,
   But then I shall understand, as all along I
    have myself been understood.
Thus 'faith and hope and love last on, these
    three,' but the greatest of all is love.

1 Corinthians 13 Moffatt

EPIPHANY

Unclench your fists
Hold out your hands.
Take mine.
Let us hold each other.
Thus is his Glory
Manifest.

Madeleine L'Engle